CREATED BY EVERYDAY PSALMIST

_____

The Everyday Psalmist

A GUIDED JOURNAL FOR GETTING REAL WITH GOD

Ink &
Willow

Contents

LIFE IS HARD

GOD'S GOT THIS

Introduction

The next time you hear someone pray aloud in public, pay close attention to the language being used. Not always, but quite often, you'll hear words and phrases that are different from those we use in daily conversations with our coworkers, or during Friday-night get-togethers with friends, or on Sunday-evening phone calls to relatives. What you're hearing is what pastor and poet Eugene Peterson called "godtalk," an impersonal language to talk about or even to God. Godtalk is speech that ends up feeling like insider language, like a secret code consisting of the right words and phrases that only certain people have access to while the rest of us don't. And occasions like public prayers are notorious for being full of it.

It's not that there aren't some words and phrases that naturally find a place in our prayers, but it's that godtalk sounds, for lack of a better word, *polished*. And because you hear it most often spoken by respected voices when it comes to matters of faith and spirituality—people who appear to have everything together—it's not a stretch to say that godtalk can be a little, if not a lot, intimidating. The end result of such talk is that far too many people consider prayer, and maybe even God, a subject best left to the experts and/or the insiders. And that's simply not true. Prayer is not a gated community.

The New Testament book of Luke (4:18–19, ESV) records Jesus quoting these words:

> *"The Spirit of the Lord is upon me,*
> *because he has anointed me*
> *to proclaim good news to the poor.*
> *He has sent me to proclaim liberty to the captives*
> *and recovering of sight to the blind,*
> *to set at liberty those who are oppressed,*
> *to proclaim the year of the Lord's favor."*

The poor. The captives. The blind. Those who are oppressed. Think about that both literally and figuratively. God's good news, which includes this amazing gift known as prayer, is precisely for those who don't have it all together—which, if we're honest, is all of us. Prayer is universal access.

Is there some kind of antidote or resistance to this godtalk? Yes, you're in luck, for we have the gift of the biblical book of Psalms—a collection of 150 poems, songs, and prayers written over hundreds of years by a handful of authors that covers the spectrum of human experiences and emotions— from the happy to the sad to the joyful to the bittersweet to the grateful to the whiny to the angry-shaking-your-fists-at-the-sky to the down-on-hands-and-knees-whispering-please. As Eugene Peterson, the beloved translator of *The Message Bible*, explains, one of the first things we realize is that in prayer "anything goes."[1]

---

1   Eugene H. Peterson, *Eat This Book* (Grand Rapids: Wm. B. Eerdmans Publishing, 2006), 105.

Don't miss that phrase: "anything goes."

Although many English translations present otherwise, the language originally used in the Psalms (Hebrew) is a far cry from polished. The psalms in their intended language are raw, earthy, honest, personal, and from time to time just downright awkward. This is language not from people who have their lives all together, but rather from those getting everything in their lives out in the open before God.[2] While we're at it, that's a good working definition of prayer—"Getting everything out in the open before God."

The psalms teach us the language of prayer. If we learn the language, then we can begin to see that God's interested in every bit of life—nothing's off limits. Nothing. Remember, "anything goes." Everything is a context for prayer. And if we learn the language, we'll realize that the only thing we need to pray our own psalms—to pray our own prayers—is honesty. No polish, no insider language, no secret handshake, no ducks all in a row. Just honesty. If we learn the language, then we're on our way to following the apostle Paul's encouragement to "pray without ceasing" (1 Thessalonians 5:17, ESV). In other words, living a life of constant prayer.

PLEASE NOTE: Learning to write your own psalms is not intended to be a substitute for reading and praying the biblical psalms, but rather a practice to complement the discipline that has been a part of the lives of Christians for centuries.

---

2   Eugene H. Peterson, *The Message* (Colorado Springs: NavPress), 24.

WHO WROTE ALL THIS?

When asked who wrote all the psalms, most people with even a faint knowledge of them will probably mention David, the shepherd boy who killed Goliath and then grew up to be one of the most memorable kings of Israel—someone Scripture refers to as "a man after God's own heart" (1 Samuel 13). And they would be right, since David is indicated as the author of at least seventy-three of the psalms.

But while King David wrote many, he didn't write them all. Additional contributors include Solomon (one of King David's sons), Ethan and Heman (two extraordinarily wise men), Asaph (one of David's chief musicians/worship leaders), Moses (best known for his role in delivering God's people from slavery under Pharaoh), and the Sons of Korah (descendants of a rebellious contemporary in the days of Moses). In other words, the psalms were written by a variety of people, from royalty to the rebellious. And yes, some are attributed to "anonymous," a category that is broad enough to cover the rest of us. We all can contribute a verse.

THINK IN THREES

During the first few centuries AD, the psalms were arranged and divided into five different books to mirror the Pentateuch—the first five books of the Old Testament: Genesis, Exodus, Leviticus, Numbers, and Deuteronomy.

> Book I: Chapters 1–41
> Book II: Chapters 42–72

Over time, however, others have moved away from the five-books approach and arranged the psalms differently. These newer structures aren't right or wrong, simply different. A longstanding approach has been to arrange them by seven types of prayers: Lament (psalms crying out to God over grief or injustice), Thanksgiving, Enthronement (psalms affirming God's kingly reign), Pilgrimage, Royal (psalms focused on the spiritual role of God's chosen leaders), Wisdom, and Imprecatory (psalms invoking God's judgment). There's also a four-types approach: Individual Praise, Communal Praise, Individual Laments, and Communal Laments. Fives, sevens, fours, and the lists go on. Again, these are simply different ways of looking at the same material.

For this journal, you're invited to think in threes. In his book *Praying the Psalms*, scholar Walter Brueggemann suggests that our faith moves through three phases, all three of which are covered in the book of Psalms: "(a) being securely oriented; (b) being painfully disoriented; (c) being surprisingly reoriented." Popular author Anne Lamott contends that all prayer essentially boils down to three words: *Help. Thanks. Wow* (see her book by the same name). And theologian Frederick Buechner offers this gem of a quote: "Here is the world. Beautiful and terrible things will happen. Don't be afraid. I am with you."[3]

---

3   Frederick Buechner, *Beyond Words* (San Francisco: HarperSanFrancisco, 2004), 139.

Following the pattern of thought suggested by Brueg-gemann and Lamott and Buechner, this journal is divided into three sections that focus on unique responses to different types of psalms. Buechner's quote will actually frame the sections:

LIFE IS BEAUTIFUL—"beautiful things will happen"
LIFE IS HARD—"terrible things will happen"
GOD'S GOT THIS—"don't be afraid. I am with you"

Each section will provide seven examples of biblical psalms for you to read. There will be space following for you to write down your response to those particular psalms: how they make you feel, what you like, what you possibly don't like, what sensations the phrases evoke, or what memories might be stirred by the words. There are no right or wrong answers; however, remember the key: *honesty.* The same is true for the "Get Real" sections, which will invite you to recognize the beautiful, hard, and desperate moments in your own life. Treat these pages as your space for getting real with God, whether through words, drawings, or a mix of both.

The remaining parts of each section will be filled with a brief prompt to get you started so you can try writing a psalm all on your own. You won't be graded. There's not even a pass or fail. But again, the lasting benefit comes from being honest.

A NOTE ON TRANSLATIONS

Each time a psalm is introduced, the Bible version it is taken from will be noted, unless the translation is NIV (the "primary" translation used in this book). Variety is the intent here, to offer a range of how different translators have used different language to say the same thing. People often feel strongly about biblical translations, and that's fair. But remember the goal of this journal. It is not to sway you to a particular version of the Bible, but rather to guide you in learning the language of prayer so as to enrich and broaden your own prayer life going forward.

ONE LAST THING

As you move through this journal, take your time, go slowly, and don't hurry. This is not a race, but a life-giving practice. Eugene Peterson's words guide us here:

> *Mobs of words run out of our mouths, nonstop, trampling the grassy and sacred silence. We only stop when breathless. Why do we talk so much? Why do we talk so fast? Hurry is a form of violence practiced on time. But time is sacred. The purpose of language is not to murder the silence but to enter it, cautiously and reverently. Silence is not what is left over when there is nothing more to say but the aspect of time that gives meaning to sound. The poem restores silence to language so that words, organic and living, once again are given time to pulse and breathe.*[4]

4   Eugene H. Peterson, *Answering God* (New York: HarperCollins), 60.

Life is
Bea

Here is the world. Beautiful...
things will happen.

— Frederick Buechner

Enter his gates with
thanksgiving and his
courts with praise!

Psalm 100:4

As you enter this journaling experience and begin to pen your own poems and prayers, follow the guide of Psalm 100 and do it with thanksgiving and praise! Far from some manufactured "just put on a happy face" mentality, the psalmist is encouraging a more intentional mindset and a firm decision to ensure that the first steps you take into these pages are centered around thankfulness. Because yes, life is beautiful.

SHORT IS GOOD

Psalm 117 (MSG)

¹⁻² Praise GOD, everybody!
Applaud GOD, all people!
His love has taken over our lives;
GOD's faithful ways are eternal.
　　Hallelujah!

Psalm 117 (ESV)

¹ Praise the LORD, all nations!
　　Extol him, all peoples!

² For great is his steadfast love toward us,
　　and the faithfulness of the LORD endures forever.
Praise the LORD!

Psalm 117 is the shortest of the psalms. Just two
verses, but they pack quite a punch. Two translations
are presented here to give you a sense of different
approaches to the same truth.

Which of the two versions do you prefer?

_____

Why do you prefer one over the other? Is it the language? Word choices?
How it sounds to the ear?

_____

_____

_____

_____

_____

_____

_____

_____

_____

_____

IT MIGHT INTEREST YOU TO KNOW

Psalm 117 is not only
the shortest psalm but also the
shortest chapter in the Bible.

GETTING REAL

What's beautiful today?

_____

_____

What's hard right now?

_____

_____

Where do you need God most?

_____

_____

Get real with God by writing or sketching out your thoughts or feelings.

Your Turn

Short is good. And when it comes to writing your own psalm, starting out short is wise, especially if the thought of doing such a thing is relatively new for you. Based on your preferred version earlier, try your hand at writing a two-verse psalm. Just two verses, five brief lines. Approach it this way: *If I were to say what the psalmist is saying, how would I say it?* Some of your word choices may be the same. Then again, some may not. Either way is okay.

I think we delight to praise
what we enjoy because
the praise not merely
expresses but completes
the enjoyment....Fully
to enjoy is to glorify. In
commanding us to glorify
Him, God is inviting us to
enjoy Him.

C. S. LEWIS,
Reflections on the Psalms

BOOM!

Psalm 145:3–8 (NASB)

A PSALM OF PRAISE, OF DAVID.

³ Great is the LORD, and highly to be praised;
   And His greatness is unsearchable.
⁴ One generation will praise Your works to another,
   And will declare Your mighty acts.
⁵ On the glorious splendor of Your majesty
   And on Your wonderful works, I will meditate.
⁶ People will speak of the power of Your awesome acts,
   And I will tell of Your greatness.
⁷ They will burst forth in speaking of Your abundant goodness,
   And will shout joyfully of Your righteousness.

⁸ The LORD is gracious and compassionate;
   Slow to anger and great in mercy.

The psalmist says the people "burst forth" in praise. What's the first thing that comes to mind when you hear the word "burst"?

_____

_____

_____

_____

_____

Did you think bubble? A balloon? A piñata? Or maybe a garden full of hollyhocks in bloom? Essentially, something explodes—_boom_! If you were to "burst forth" or boom with praise to God for something—anything at all—what's the first thing that crosses your mind?

_____

_____

_____

_____

_____

_____

Now hold that thought. Verse 4 reads, "One generation will praise Your works to another." Who is someone of another generation you can share that praise with? _____

_____

_____

_____

_____

_____

_____

One of the things the psalmist is grateful for is stated in verse 8: The Lord is "slow to anger and great in mercy."

There may not be a lot of them, but chances are good you've had at least one experience of someone being slow to anger and great in mercy toward you. Take a few minutes and reflect on that encounter. What effect did that experience have on you? Have you been able to pay that grace forward in any way?

_____

_____

_____

_____

_____

_____

_____

_____

_____

_____

It Might Interest You to Know

Psalm 145 is the only
psalm that designates itself as
a "psalm of praise."

GETTING REAL

What's beautiful today?

_____

_____

What's hard right now?

_____

_____

Where do you need God most?

_____

_____

Get real with God by writing or sketching out your thoughts or feelings.

Your Turn

If you're a bit behind in giving gratitude (aren't we all?), here's your chance to catch up by writing your own psalm of thanksgiving to God by describing your experience with that "slow to anger, great in mercy" person. Use the space below to add the name of the person and the experience you had, going into as much or as little detail as you choose. You can write it in paragraph form, or you could write verses much like the psalmist. Don't worry about writing it wrong. You can't, if you're being honest with yourself before God.

Psalm 145 begins like this:

I will exalt You, my God, the King,

And I will bless Your name forever and ever.

I will bless You for _____

_____

_____

_____

_____

_____

_____

_____

_____

_____

_____

_____

TO RECOGNIZE THAT
THE PSALMS CALL US TO
PRAY AND SING AT THE
INTERSECTIONS OF THE
TIMES—OF OUR TIME AND
GOD'S TIME, OF THE THEN,
THE NOW, AND THE NOT
YET—IS TO UNDERSTAND
HOW THOSE EMOTIONS ARE
TO BE HELD WITHIN THE
RHYTHM OF A LIFE LIVED IN
GOD'S PRESENCE.

N.T. WRIGHT,
The Case for the Psalms: Why They Are Essential

AWE AND WONDER

Psalm 8 (KJV)
A PSALM OF DAVID

1 O LORD, our Lord, how excellent is thy name in all the earth! who hast set thy glory above the heavens.

2 Out of the mouth of babes and sucklings hast thou ordained strength because of thine enemies, that thou mightest still the enemy and the avenger.

3 When I consider thy heavens, the work of thy fingers, the moon and the stars, which thou hast ordained;

4 What is man, that thou art mindful of him? and the son of man, that thou visitest him?

5 For thou hast made him a little lower than the angels, and hast crowned him with glory and honour.

6 Thou madest him to have dominion over the works of thy hands; thou hast put all things under his feet:

7 All sheep and oxen, yea, and the beasts of the field;

8 The fowl of the air, and the fish of the sea, and whatsoever passeth through the paths of the seas.

9 O LORD our Lord, how excellent is thy name in all the earth!

What words or phrases got your attention as you read this psalm?

_____

_____

_____

_____

Now, what about those phrases caused you to focus in on them? Was it the word choice itself? Something about how the word or phrase was used? Did anything stir a thought about this psalm that you've not had before?

_____

_____

_____

_____

_____

_____

_____

_____

It Might Interest You to Know

The short story "That Thou Art Mindful of Him" by science fiction author Isaac Asimov is taken from the phrase found in Psalm 8.

GETTING REAL

What's beautiful today?

_____

_____

What's hard right now?

_____

_____

Where do you need God most?

_____

_____

Get real with God by writing or sketching out your thoughts or feelings.

Your Turn

Now it's your turn. Using Psalm 8 as a prompt (feel free to look back at it and mimic David's words, since that's how we learn), allow your mind to take an honest inventory of all the things you sense around you or the things that wow you. Pay attention and think nouns—persons, places, things. You may sense some big, significant things. You may also sense smaller, rather ordinary things, but they're just as meaningful. Sit with your thoughts for a minute, and then write a response of thankfulness in light of what you see and hear and smell and taste and touch (your senses are good guides here).

A Psalm of _____

(fill in the blank above with your name—it's yours, after all!)

O Lord our God, when I look around me and see _____

_____

_____

_____

_____

_____

In light of all that, _____

_____

_____

_____

_____

_____

"Delight yourself in the Lord; and He will give you the desires of your heart" (Psalm 37:4). This doesn't mean that He's necessarily giving you what you want, but rather that He is in the process of transforming your soul to desire what He wants.

PRISCILLA SHIRER,
Discerning the Voice of God

WHERE'D YOU COME FROM?

Psalm 100:3, 5 (ESV)

³ Know that the LORD, he is God!
   It is he who made us, and we are his;
   we are his people, and the sheep of his pasture.

⁵ For the LORD is good;
   his steadfast love endures forever,
   and his faithfulness to all generations.

Identity—where you came from, who your people are, who you are—the answers feel weighty to each of us for different reasons. If asked, how would you respond to the questions below? Granted, that last one is a bit tougher than the first two, but give it a shot.

1. Where are you from?

_____

_____

2. Who are your people?

_____

_____

3. Who are you?

_____

_____

It Might Interest You to Know

Ralph Vaughan Williams
composed a piece for Queen
Elizabeth's coronation in 1953
based on "The Old Hundredth Psalm
Tune" (as in Psalm 100).

GETTING REAL

What's beautiful today?

_____

_____

What's hard right now?

_____

_____

Where do you need God most?

_____

_____

Get real with God by writing or sketching out your thoughts or feelings.

Your Turn

The author of Psalm 100 declared an eternal truth:

God made us. We are his. We are his people. But that doesn't negate those earthbound answers you gave earlier. Write a psalm of thanksgiving based on your answers to the questions "Where are you from?" and "Who are your people?" It might sound something like this:

Lord, I know that you are God,
that I am yours, a sheep of your pasture.
I also know that you rooted me in central Oklahoma,
the daughter of a single-mom schoolteacher.
That was not by accident, Lord. Thank you.

That's just one example of how you could humbly give thanks for where you're from. Go ahead, give it a try.

A Psalm of _____

_____

_____

_____

_____

_____

_____

_____

_____

_____

[THE PSALMS] BECOME
LIKE A MIRROR TO THE
PERSON SINGING THEM, SO
THAT HE MIGHT PERCEIVE
HIMSELF AND THE EMOTIONS
OF HIS SOUL. UNDER ALL THE
CIRCUMSTANCES OF LIFE,
WE SHALL FIND THAT THESE
DIVINE SONGS SUIT OURSELVES
AND MEET OUR OWN SOULS'
NEED AT EVERY TURN.

SAINT ATHANASIUS,
On the Incarnation

ALL IN

Psalm 111:1–5 (ESV)

[1] Praise the LORD!
  I will give thanks to the LORD with my whole heart,
    in the company of the upright, in the congregation.

[2] Great are the works of the LORD,
    studied by all who delight in them.

[3] Full of splendor and majesty is his work,
    and his righteousness endures forever.

[4] He has caused his wondrous works to be remembered;
    the LORD is gracious and merciful.

[5] He provides food for those who fear him;
    he remembers his covenant forever.

What's the last thing you recall doing half-heartedly? No shame here, as all of us had/have/will have such moments. But what's the most recent time? And if you can, pinpoint why it was a half-hearted attempt.

_____

_____

_____

_____

_____

_____

_____

_____

_____

Now, what have you done recently that was wholehearted? Like you were all in or in full-send mode?

_____

_____

_____

_____

_____

_____

_____

_____

_____

_____

The psalmist speaks as an individual—"*I* will give thanks"— but the gratitude occurs in the context of others, "the congregation." What would it look like for you to give wholehearted thanks to God in the presence of others? What's an example of an "odds are good I would actually try it" scenario?

_____

_____

_____

_____

_____

_____

_____

_____

_____

_____

It Might Interest You to Know

Psalm 111 is an acrostic
poem. It consists of twenty-two
phrases (excluding verse 1a),
each of which begins with a successive
letter of the Hebrew alphabet.

GETTING REAL

What's beautiful today?

_____

_____

What's hard right now?

_____

_____

Where do you need God most?

_____

_____

Get real with God by writing or sketching out your thoughts or feelings.

Do you ever make lists before you go shopping? Experts tell us lists keep us focused. A list ensures we don't forget something and, maybe just as importantly, keeps us from ending up in the checkout lane with a number of items we really don't need.

To write your own psalm of wholehearted gratitude, simply make a list of the things you're thankful for. It's not any less of a psalm than lines of verse or paragraphs of prose. Don't hold back. Go wholehearted, all in, full send. (And if you want more parameters, try creating your list as an acrostic, with each line starting with a successive letter of the alphabet.)

A Psalm of _____

- _____
- _____
- _____
- _____
- _____
- _____
- _____
- _____
- _____
- _____
- _____
- _____
- _____

Prayer does not mean simply to pour out one's heart. It means rather to find the way to God and to speak with him, whether the heart is full or empty. No man can do that by himself. For that he needs Jesus Christ.

DIETRICH BONHOEFFER,
Psalms: The Prayer Book of the Bible

THE HERO OF YOUR STORY

Psalm 146:1–7 (RSV)

[1] Praise the LORD!
  Praise the LORD, O my soul!
[2] I will praise the LORD as long as I live;
    I will sing praises to my God while I have being.

[3] Put not your trust in princes,
    in a son of man, in whom there is no help.
[4] When his breath departs he returns to his earth;
    on that very day his plans perish.

[5] Happy is he whose help is the God of Jacob,
    whose hope is in the LORD his God,
[6] who made heaven and earth,
    the sea, and all that is in them;
    who keeps faith for ever;
[7] who executes justice for the oppressed;
    who gives food to the hungry.

In a time when we all too often look to ourselves or others to be the heroes of our stories, the charge from the psalmist might sound countercultural: our help and hope is the God of Jacob.

It's not that we can't put hope in flesh and blood, but at the end of the day, the hero of humanity's story is God. Where or in whom have you previously placed hope that ended in disappointment, or possibly even heartbreak? Be as specific as you can.

_____

_____

_____

_____

_____

_____

_____

_____

_____

_____

_____

_____

_____

_____

_____

_____

_____

_____

Take note of the word used in verse 5 to describe the state of being of someone who trusts in God. Such a person is described as

_____

_____

_____

_____

_____

_____

_____

In Christian circles, a common argument is that joy is preferable to happiness, since joy is often described as being deeper or more lasting while happiness is denoted as shallower or more fleeting. But the book of Psalms (e.g., 41, 33, 34, 65, 83, 89, 94, and 106) frequently uses the Hebrew word a*sh'reh*, which means "content" or "satisfied," for what we usually refer to as "happy."

It Might Interest You to Know

Psalm 146 is one of six psalms that include the phrase "O my soul." The psalmist is essentially preaching to himself.

GETTING REAL

What's beautiful today?

_____

_____

What's hard right now?

_____

_____

Where do you need God most?

_____

_____

Get real with God by writing or sketching out your thoughts or feelings.

Your Turn

Use verses 5–7 of Psalm 146 as a template for your psalm, taking an almost fill-in-the-blank approach to get yourself started. By no means do you have to stay in that form, but start there. The goal is to personalize the psalm and make it specific to your life and your experience while also keeping it in the vein of thanksgiving and gratitude. Take your time, try and try again, and play around with it until you've got something that feels true to the spirit of the original psalm (God is our hero) while also speaking to what you've experienced in your own life.

Once you've filled out the template, use the next page to try your hand at creating your own psalm from scratch. You've got this!

A Psalm of _____

5 Happy is [the one] whose _____ is the God of Jacob,

whose _____ is in the Lord [their] God,

6 who made _____ and _____ ,

the _____ , and all that is in them;

who keeps _____ for ever;

7 who executes _____ for the _____ ;

who gives _____ to the _____ .

A Psalm of _____

There's something about lifting your voice to God, especially in the words of the Psalms. If you have something to be thankful for, it gives shape to your gratefulness. And if you don't, the song becomes a place into which to pour your overflowing heart. The psalms give voice to your sorrow and pain, and singing them lifts up your heart. It resets your focus on God and gives you hope.

SARAH CHRISTMYER,

Becoming Women of the Word: How to Answer God's Call with Purpose and Joy

SOLID

[1] Come, let us sing for joy to the LORD;
    let us shout aloud to the Rock of our salvation.
[2] Let us come before him with thanksgiving
    and extol him with music and song.

[3] For the LORD is the great God,
    the great King above all gods.
[4] In his hand are the depths of the earth,
    and the mountain peaks belong to him.
[5] The sea is his, for he made it,
    and his hands formed the dry land.

[6] Come, let us bow down in worship,
    let us kneel before the LORD our Maker;
[7] for he is our God
    and we are the people of his pasture,
    the flock under his care.

In verse 1, the psalmist uses a phrase for God that has become a touchstone for believers over the years— "the Rock of our salvation." Maybe it's a stretch for you to consider God as "rock." But what about another word that captures that same meaning, like "solid"?

List three things in your life right now that you would describe as solid.

_____

_____

_____

Was God on your list? Why did or why didn't God make the cut?

_____

_____

_____

_____

_____

_____

It Might Interest You to Know

While Psalm 95 has no author attribution, Hebrews 4:7 attributes it to David.

GETTING REAL

What's beautiful today?

_____

_____

What's hard right now?

_____

_____

Where do you need God most?

_____

_____

Get real with God by writing or sketching out your thoughts or feelings.

Your Turn

Maybe God didn't make your list due to circumstances or situations in your life right now that seem unfair, unjust, or just downright horrible. Or maybe it wasn't so much that God didn't make the list as it is that your faith in God is the thing that's shaky. Notice the underlined text below, where the psalmist gives thanks for realities beyond his own immediate life, such as aspects of the created order—

⁴ In his hand are <u>the depths of the earth</u>,
   and <u>the mountain peaks</u> belong to him.
⁵ <u>The sea</u> is his, for he made it,
   and his hands formed <u>the dry land</u>.

—as opposed to interior realities, such as physical health or financial issues.

As you try your hand at writing your own version of this psalm, consider writing it in the form of a letter (yes, a "Dear God" note). As you begin, give thanks in your own words for those things that are solid in our world. Let the middle of your note honestly reflect on those unsolid realities in your life. And conclude by returning to a place of gratitude for the Maker of our world, who is also the Maker of you.

A Psalm of _____

Dear God,

_____
_____
_____
_____
_____
_____
_____
_____
_____
_____
_____
_____
_____
_____
_____
_____
_____
_____
_____
_____
_____
_____

Sincerely,

_____

Life is

Ha

rdf

Here is the world . . . terrible things will happen.

—Frederick Buechner

How long, LORD?
Will you hide yourself forever?
How long will your wrath burn like fire? . . .
Who can live and not see death,
or who can escape the power of the grave?
Lord, where is your former great love,
which in your faithfulness you
swore to David?

Psalm 89:46, 48–49

Yes, life is beautiful. And life is also hard. In fact, some days it's terrible. Wars and rumors of wars, the daily hemorrhage of news, and more injustices and abuses than we can keep up with, both in our individual lives and in the greater communal circle of humanity. To our benefit, the Psalms do not sidestep this hard and often terrible reality. Rather, they fall in step beside us and encourage us to *lament*—to mourn or grieve. The lament psalms are the individual and corporate cries of God's people. The cry then, and now, is visceral—"How long, O Lord?"

C'MON, LORD. HOW LONG?

Psalm 13 (ESV)

TO THE CHOIRMASTER. A PSALM OF DAVID.

[1] How long, O LORD? Will you forget me forever?
    How long will you hide your face from me?
[2] How long must I take counsel in my soul
    and have sorrow in my heart all the day?
How long shall my enemy be exalted over me?

[3] Consider and answer me, O LORD my God;
    light up my eyes, lest I sleep the sleep of death,
[4] lest my enemy say, "I have prevailed over him,"
    lest my foes rejoice because I am shaken.

[5] But I have trusted in your steadfast love;
    my heart shall rejoice in your salvation.
[6] I will sing to the LORD,
    because he has dealt bountifully with me.

"How long, O Lord?" We've all said it, probably on numerous occasions, and for a host of reasons. Something isn't right, things are out of sort, or we feel like we're at the end of our rope. And sometimes, much to our dismay, the wrong thing or things often look or sound or feel like an experience we've been through before—making us feel forgotten, even abandoned, with an aching heart. The details are always different, but that feeling is the same. And here it is again.

What was your most recent experience of "How long, Lord?"

_____

_____

_____

_____

_____

_____

_____

_____

_____

_____

_____

_____

_____

_____

_____

_____

_____

_____

_____

_____

_____

The psalmist uses rather evocative words and phrases here to communicate that this tragedy is more than stubbing a toe or forgetting to take the trash to the curb. The "sleep of death" sounds threatening, right? And he is "shaken"—a word that lands somewhere in the vicinity of violence. Now think back to the experience you listed on the opposite page. What words or phrases would you use to describe your experience?

_____

_____

_____

_____

_____

_____

_____

_____

_____

It Might Interest You to Know

Charles Spurgeon,
an English Baptist preacher
in the late nineteenth century
who was known as "The Prince
of Preachers," referred to Psalm 13
as the "Howling Psalm."

GETTING REAL

What's beautiful today?

_____

_____

What's hard right now?

_____

_____

Where do you need God most?

_____

_____

Get real with God by writing or sketching out your thoughts or feelings.

Your Turn

Depending on everything from your age to your family of origin to your personality traits, lament can be quite natural or extremely challenging. As you get started with your first psalm of lament, try the stream-of-consciousness approach. Use the prompt "How long, O Lord?" and then spill your guts, so to speak. You can use the experience you wrote about in the previous section for inspiration, or you can choose to write about another one. Don't worry about punctuation or format, just write a paragraph of lament. And remember that the very thing you might be hesitant to put down on paper may in fact be the very thing that needs to move out of your head or heart and into the light of God's listening ears.

A Psalm of _____

How long, O Lord?

_____

_____

_____

_____

_____

_____

_____

_____

_____

_____

_____

_____

_____

_____

_____

When we are in the darkness, we begin to feel like we have always been there. But it is not true. David reminds himself that God has been faithful in the past; God will be faithful again. He urges himself to put his hope in God because the morning will come.

JOHN ELDREDGE,

Moving Mountains: How You, God, and Prayer Can Change Things for Good

I'M DROWNING HERE

Psalm 25:1–2; 16–20 (TLB)

[1] To you, O Lord, I pray.

[2] Don't fail me, Lord, for I am trusting you. Don't let my enemies succeed. Don't give them victory over me.
[16] Come, Lord, and show me your mercy, for I am helpless, overwhelmed, in deep distress; [17] my problems go from bad to worse. Oh, save me from them all! [18] See my sorrows; feel my pain; forgive my sins. [19] See how many enemies I have and how viciously they hate me! [20] Save me from them! Deliver my life from their power! Oh, let it never be said that I trusted you in vain!

Helpless. Overwhelmed. In deep distress. Sorrow. Pain. Sins. Problems going from bad to worse. Sound familiar? Feel familiar? In the middle of all that, the psalmist's cry is essentially "See me! Save me!"

Describe the last time you felt helpless and overwhelmed. It might have been something epic, or it might have been something rather small. But likely, whatever it was probably still made you feel like you were drowning, and like nobody was paying attention.

_____

_____

_____

_____

_____

_____

_____

_____

_____

It Might Interest You to Know

The Psalms are often considered to be the "Bible within the Bible," or the *Tehillim*, since they contain all the major themes of the biblical narrative.

GETTING REAL

What's beautiful today?

_____

_____

What's hard right now?

_____

_____

Where do you need God most?

_____

_____

Get real with God by writing or sketching out your thoughts or feelings.

Your Turn

Using the psalmist's verse structure, fill in the blanks with your own words. Imagine you're waving your arms for dear life, trying to get God's attention. What would you say (scream)?

A Psalm of _____

Come, Lord, and show me your mercy,

for I am helpless, _____ ,

in deep _____ ;

my problems go from _____ .

Oh, save me from them all!

See my _____ ;

feel my _____ ;

forgive my sin of _____ .

See how many enemies I have? And how viciously they hate me?

Save me from _____ !

Deliver my life from _____ !

The psalmist is
brutally honest about
the explosive joy
that he's feeling and
the deep sorrow or
confusion, and it's that
that sets the Psalms
apart for me. And I
often think, gosh, well,
why isn't church music
more like that?

BONO,

"Bono & Eugene Peterson: The Psalms"

GET UP, GOD! WAKE UP!

Psalm 44:9–16; 23 (MSG)

⁹⁻¹² But now you've walked off and left us,
  you've disgraced us and won't fight for us.
You made us turn tail and run;
  those who hate us have cleaned us out.
You delivered us as sheep to the butcher,
  you scattered us to the four winds.
You sold your people at a discount—
  you made nothing on the sale.

¹³⁻¹⁶ You made people on the street,
  people we know, poke fun and call us names.
You made us a joke among the godless,
  a cheap joke among the rabble.
Every day I'm up against it,
  my nose rubbed in my shame—
Gossip and ridicule fill the air,
  people out to get me crowd the street.

²³ Get up, GOD! Are you going to sleep all day?
  Wake up! Don't you care what happens to us?

Consider this line: "Get up, God! Are you going to sleep all day?"

On a scale of 1–5 (5 being most comfortable), how comfortable are you saying that to God? _____

If your rating was 1–3, what informs your level of discomfort? Do you feel such a statement is disrespectful? Inappropriate? Crosses some sort of line? A combination of all these? Be honest. If your rating was higher, describe a time recently when you felt like saying those words.

_____

_____

_____

_____

_____

_____

_____

_____

It Might Interest You to Know

Psalm 44 is attributed to the sons of Korah. Korah was a cousin to Moses, and his descendants represented an important branch of singers.

GETTING REAL

What's beautiful today?

_____

_____

What's hard right now?

_____

_____

Where do you need God most?

_____

_____

Get real with God by writing or sketching out your thoughts or feelings.

Your Turn

Go back and read through the excerpt from Psalm 44. Take your time. This is not an individual lament (I/me), but rather a communal one (we/us). And the blame or accusation? That's directed solely at God.

Regardless of how you earlier scored on the comfortability spectrum, try your hand at giving God a piece of your mind—not so much as an individual but as a member of a group (the possibilities here are endless). Keep the "us" in mind.

A Psalm of _____

Get up, God! Are you going to sleep all day?
    Wake up! Don't you care what happens to us?

_____

_____

_____

_____

_____

_____

_____

_____

_____

_____

Get up and come to our rescue.
    If you love us so much, *Help us!*

THE PSALMS, THEN, ARE
FOR THOSE WHO KNOW
THAT THEY SPEND MUCH
OF THEIR LIFE HIDING
SECRETS; THEY ARE ALSO
FOR THOSE WHO KNOW
THAT STANDING IN THE
PRESENCE OF GOD "IS THE
ONE PLACE WHERE SUCH
SECRETS CANNOT AND
MUST NOT BE HIDDEN."

WALTER BRUEGGEMANN,
Whom No Secrets Are Hid: Introducing the Psalms

WHY?

Psalm 22:1–2 (ESV)

¹ My God, my God, why have you forsaken me?
  Why are you so far from saving me, from the
  words of my groaning?
² O my God, I cry by day, but you do not answer,
  and by night, but I find no rest.

It Might Interest You to Know

The first line of Psalm 22 was
part of the "last words" Jesus spoke
from the cross before he died.

Why? It's easily one of a child's favorite questions to ask (repeatedly) as she grows and learns more about the world in which she finds herself. Of course, the question doesn't diminish as we grow older, but the hopes of a satisfactory answer certainly do. When have you asked God "why" recently?

_____
_____
_____

Godforsaken. Who/what/where immediately comes to mind when you hear that word?

_____
_____
_____
_____

The psalmist keeps crying, by day and night, but there is no answer. There are days and weeks and months in our lives when the questions we ask have no answers. Those seasons can be challenging, but reading the words of this psalm can help remind us that our experiences are not abnormal "glitches" when it comes to faith. We're all in the waiting together. When have you been in a waiting season and needed the words of this psalm?

_____
_____
_____
_____
_____

GETTING REAL

What's beautiful today?

_____

_____

What's hard right now?

_____

_____

Where do you need God most?

_____

_____

Get real with God by writing or sketching out your thoughts or feelings.

Your Turn

Why? You've asked it before, and you'll no doubt ask it again. Take some time and write out your *whys*. Separate them by commas, semicolons, dashes—anything to represent continuous honesty and openness before God.

A Psalm of _____

My God, my God, why _____

_____

_____

_____

_____

_____

_____

_____

_____

_____

_____

_____

_____

_____

_____

_____

_____

_____

The psalms enable us to bring into our conversation with God feelings and thoughts most of us think we need to get rid of before God will be interested in hearing from us.

ELLEN DAVIS,
*Getting Involved with God: Rediscovering
the Old Testament*

HARD THINGS

Psalm 60:1–3 (ESV)

TO THE CHOIRMASTER: ACCORDING TO SHUSHAN EDUTH.
A *MIKTAM* OF DAVID; FOR INSTRUCTION; WHEN HE STROVE
WITH ARAM-NAHARAIM AND WITH ARAM-ZOBAH, AND WHEN
JOAB ON HIS RETURN STRUCK DOWN TWELVE THOUSAND
OF EDOM IN THE VALLEY OF SALT.

[1] O God, you have rejected us, broken our defenses;
    you have been angry; oh, restore us.
[2] You have made the land to quake; you have torn it open;
    repair its breaches, for it totters.
[3] You have made your people see hard things;
    you have given us wine to drink that made us stagger.

The phrase is a bit old-fashioned now, but people used to talk about "falling on hard times." Words or phrases that are synonymous include "dark times," "fall from grace," and "rough patch." And while these phrases usually refer to financial difficulties, they by no means are limited to money.

Here, the psalmist indicates God has shown or made the people see and experience "hard things," some of them staggering. List three things you've been a witness to that could be described by the phrase "hard things." This is another communal lament, so think not so much *what I've seen* as *what we've seen.*

1. _____

_____

2. _____

_____

3. _____

_____

It Might Interest You to Know

Psalm 60 is the last psalm of six *Miktams* (see page 99). Potential meanings for this word include (1) an inscription on a pillar; or (2) an inscription in gold, since the root of the word means "gold."

GETTING REAL

What's beautiful today?

_____

_____

What's hard right now?

_____

_____

Where do you need God most?

_____

_____

Get real with God by writing or sketching out your thoughts or feelings.

Your Turn

In these first three verses, David, the author of this psalm, has a recurring theme: "You have"—meaning that while there were obviously minor characters at work causing challenges in his life, the hard things could ultimately be traced back to God. When it comes to the "hard" you've witnessed, what are four things you're honestly willing to attribute to God (as David did)? Maybe there were human elements involved, but from your perspective, did it feel like God was the main character behind the scenes? Conclude your psalm by putting your own take on David's two lines (verse 3).

A Psalm of _____

O God, you have _____ .

You have _____ .

You have _____ .

You have _____ .

You have made your people see _____ .

You have given us _____ .

The Psalmist's "I" accommodates a vast congregation of individuals and groups down the centuries around the world today. They are all somehow embraced in this "I." A vast array of stories, situations, sufferings, blessings, joys, and deaths have been read and prayed into the Psalms by those who have identified with their first person. It amounts to an extraordinarily capacious and hospitable "I."

DAVID F. FORD,
Self and Salvation: Being Transformed

THE GOOD OLD DAYS

Psalm 77:1–9 (NLT)

FOR JEDUTHUN, THE CHOIR DIRECTOR: A PSALM OF ASAPH.

[1] I cry out to God; yes, I shout.
   I am too distressed even to pray!
[2] When I was in deep trouble,
   I searched for the Lord.
 All night long I prayed, with hands lifted toward heaven,
   but my soul was not comforted.
[3] I think of God, and I moan,
   overwhelmed with longing for his help.

Interlude

[4] You don't let me sleep.
   I am too distressed even to pray!
[5] I think of the good old days,
   long since ended,
[6] when my nights were filled with joyful songs.
   I search my soul and ponder the difference now.
[7] Has the Lord rejected me forever?
   Will he never again be kind to me?
[8] Is his unfailing love gone forever?
   Have his promises permanently failed?
[9] Has God forgotten to be gracious?
   Has he slammed the door on his compassion?

"The good old days"—a phrase that can conjure up everything from cherished childhood memories to a time in your spiritual life when God felt clear, close, and concerned. What does that phrase bring to mind in relation to your family and/or friends?

_____

_____

_____

_____

_____

Now ponder that phrase as it relates to your life of faith in God. What comes to mind?

_____

_____

_____

_____

_____

It Might Interest You to Know

A characteristic of the twelve "psalms of Asaph" is the use of the word *selah* (indicated here as "interlude"). Although the exact definition of the word is unclear, most commentators believe it indicates an intentional pause in the psalm— almost a moment to take a breath.

GETTING REAL

What's beautiful today?

_____

_____

What's hard right now?

_____

_____

Where do you need God most?

_____

_____

Get real with God by writing or sketching out your thoughts or feelings.

Your Turn

Recall a time when you were in what the psalmist calls "deep trouble." Not a time when you were in distress and a miracle fell out of the sky, but rather a time when one didn't, even though you begged and pleaded and prayed. As you keep that memory in mind, re-read verses 1–9 of Psalm 77, and then write your own nine-or-so verses in that same vein. No fill-in-the-blank or other prompt approach this time. Simply write out all the feelings and all the questions. Don't forget to take a *selah* (interlude) in the middle if you need it.

A Psalm of _____

_____

_____

_____

_____

_____

_____

_____

_____

_____

_____

_____

_____

_____

_____

_____

_____

The Psalms make it possible to say things that are otherwise unsayable. In church, they have the capacity to free us to talk about things that we cannot talk about anywhere else.

JOHN GOLDINGAY,
Psalms, Volume 1: Psalms 1–41

GET 'EM, GOD!

Psalm 79:5–10 (MSG)

⁵⁻⁷ How long do we have to put up with this, GOD?
    Do you have it in for us for good?
    Will your smoldering rage never cool down?
If you're going to be angry, be angry
    with the pagans who care nothing about you,
    or your rival kingdoms who ignore you.
They're the ones who ruined Jacob,
    who wrecked and looted the place where he lived.

⁸⁻¹⁰ Don't blame us for the sins of our parents.
    Hurry up and help us; we're at the end of our rope.
You're famous for helping; God, give *us* a break.
    Your reputation is on the line.
Pull us out of this mess, forgive us our sins—
    do what you're famous for doing!
Don't let the heathen get by with their sneers:
    "Where's your God? Is he out to lunch?"
Go public and show the godless world
    that they can't kill your servants and get by with it.

This section got started and will conclude on the same note: "How long?" Psalm 79 is a communal lament ("us" instead of "I") infused with a healthy dose of the imprecatory thrown in there as well. *Imprecatory* psalms contain curses or prayers for the punishment of one's enemies, such as in verse 10: "Don't let the heathen get by with their sneers" (MSG). The psalm continues in verse 12: "And render unto our neighbours sevenfold into their bosom their reproach, wherewith they have reproached thee, O Lord" (KJV). Yeah, yikes.

There is not consensus among scholars regarding the relevance of imprecatory psalms for believers; in other words, *should you pray them or not?* Two things to mention here:

1. Imprecatory psalms come from an experience of deep injustice against God's people. In the case of Psalm 79, the "pagans" had defiled the Temple of Jerusalem, murdered God's servants, and left their unburied bodies for the wildlife.

2. An imprecatory psalm is not prayed or spoken for people to take vengeance into their own hands, but rather to plead for God to rise up and punish the wicked.

Were you aware imprecatory psalms were in the Bible? What's your reaction to psalms like Psalm 79?

_____

_____

_____

_____

_____

_____

Do you believe such psalms are beneficial for us today? Why or why not?

_____

_____

_____

_____

_____

_____

_____

_____

_____

_____

_____

_____

_____

_____

_____

It Might Interest You to Know

The New American Bible
refers to Psalm 79 as "a psalm
for Jerusalem."

GETTING REAL

What's beautiful today?

_____

_____

What's hard right now?

_____

_____

Where do you need God most?

_____

_____

Get real with God by writing or sketching out your thoughts or feelings.

Your Turn

Remember, this is a prayer, writing, and reflection journal. Your journal. What you fill these pages with is yours. If you were to try to write an imprecatory psalm, how would you even begin? Here's an idea: "How long?" And then proceed to describe the injustices committed against a group of people. The possibilities are endless, from the numbers of victims of sexual abuse to the exhausted survivors of war to any group you're familiar with who's "been done wrong" time and time again.

A Psalm of _____

How long, Lord? _____

_____

_____

_____

_____

_____

_____

_____

_____

_____

_____

_____

_____

_____

_____

_____

_____

What happens when we pray the psalms under the light of God's grace? We become free to pray with abandonment because we have abandoned ourselves to this gracious God.

W. DAVID O. TAYLOR,

Open and Unafraid: The Psalms as a Guide to Life

God's

GOT

THIS

Here is the world. Beautiful and terrible things will happen. Don't be afraid. I am with you.

—Frederick Buechner

Whoever dwells in the shelter
of the Most High

will rest in the shadow
of the Almighty.

I will say of the LORD,
"He is my refuge and my fortress,

my God, in whom I trust."

Psalm 91:1–2

Life is beautiful, and as such calls for thanksgiving. And life is terrible, a reality which demands our honest cries for help. And God is good, as the psalmist declares: "God is our refuge and strength, a very present help in trouble" (46:1, ESV). God is always near, ever present. God is with us. Don't be afraid.

BE STILL

Psalm 46 (ESV)

TO THE CHOIRMASTER. OF THE SONS OF KORAH.
ACCORDING TO ALAMOTH. A SONG.

¹ God is our refuge and strength,
a very present help in trouble.
² Therefore we will not fear though the earth gives way,
though the mountains be moved into the heart of the sea,
³ though its waters roar and foam,
though the mountains tremble at its swelling. *Selah*

⁴ There is a river whose streams make glad the city of God,
the holy habitation of the Most High.
⁵ God is in the midst of her; she shall not be moved;
God will help her when morning dawns.
⁶ The nations rage, the kingdoms totter;
he utters his voice, the earth melts.
⁷ The LORD of hosts is with us;
the God of Jacob is our fortress. *Selah*

⁸ Come, behold the works of the LORD,
how he has brought desolations on the earth.
⁹ He makes wars cease to the end of the earth;
he breaks the bow and shatters the spear;
he burns the chariots with fire.
¹⁰ "Be still, and know that I am God.
I will be exalted among the nations,
I will be exalted in the earth!"
¹¹ The LORD of hosts is with us;
the God of Jacob is our fortress. *Selah*

Notice how the psalmist doesn't avoid the terrible realities of what he's facing. Instead, he goes to the extreme of calling them out with four "even though" statements—

²though the earth gives way,
   though the mountains be moved into the heart of the sea,
³ though its waters roar and foam,
   though the mountains tremble at its swelling.

The important fact to note, however, is that the psalmist doesn't stop there. Even as everything in the surrounding world is threatening to collapse, even in the midst of terrifying uncertainty and calamity, the powerful presence of God still holds all together as the central message of the psalm—

¹⁰ "Be still, and know that I am God."

What are some "even though" realities that are affecting your life and your peace right now?

_____

_____

_____

_____

_____

_____

_____

_____

_____

_____

What is one promise or characteristic of God that you can claim even in the midst of those realities?

_____

_____

_____

_____

The message of "be still" that God spoke over the psalmist is also true for us today. What other messages have you recently heard God speak over you?

_____

_____

_____

_____

_____

_____

It Might Interest You to Know

Martin Luther wrote the
enduring hymn "A Mighty Fortress
is Our God" based on Psalm 46.

GETTING REAL

What's beautiful today?

_____

_____

What's hard right now?

_____

_____

Where do you need God most?

_____

_____

Get real with God by writing or sketching out your thoughts or feelings.

Your Turn

"God, I will trust in you even though . . ." What extremes does your mind come up with to complete that sentence? Use the psalmist's lines as a reference but add your four extremes in the space below.

^{2} though the earth gives way,
    though the mountains be moved into the heart of the sea,
^{3} though its waters roar and foam,
    though the mountains tremble at its swelling.

A Psalm of _____

^{2} though _____,
    though _____,

^{3} though _____,
    though _____.

To "Be still, and know that I am God" can take many shapes in our lives. At least one is repeating these lines as a prayer after those extremes:

The Lord of hosts is with us;
the God of Jacob is our fortress.

What's another way for you to "be still, and know"? Write out your answer as a prayer.

Lord,

For me to be still and know looks like _____

_____

_____

_____

_____

_____

_____

_____

_____

_____

_____

_____

_____

_____

_____

_____

_____

Amen.

A JOURNEY
THROUGH
THE PSALMS IS
THE JOURNEY
OF THE LIFE
OF FAITH.

DENISE DOMBKOWSKI HOPKINS,
Journey Through the Psalms

NO FEAR

Psalm 27:1–3, 5–6; 10–14

OF DAVID.

¹ The LORD is my light and my salvation—
  whom shall I fear?
The LORD is the stronghold of my life—
  of whom shall I be afraid?
² When the wicked advance against me
  to devour me,
it is my enemies and my foes
  who will stumble and fall.
³ Though an army besiege me,
  my heart will not fear;
though war break out against me,
  even then I will be confident.

⁵ For in the day of trouble
  he will keep me safe in his dwelling;
⁶ Then my head will be exalted
  above the enemies who surround me;
at his sacred tent I will sacrifice with shouts of joy;
  I will sing and make music to the LORD.

CONTINUED ON NEXT PAGE

¹⁰ Though my father and mother forsake me,
    the LORD will receive me.
¹¹ Teach me your way, LORD;
    lead me in a straight path
    because of my oppressors.
¹² Do not turn me over to the desire of my foes,
    for false witnesses rise up against me,
    spouting malicious accusations.
¹³ I remain confident of this:
    I will see the goodness of the LORD
    in the land of the living.
¹⁴ Wait for the LORD;
    be strong and take heart
    and wait for the LORD.

For someone reading this psalm for the very first time, their takeaway impression might be that the writer is not just confident, but borders on being a little bit cocky: "whom shall I fear?" and "of whom shall I be afraid?" Those statements sound bold—brazen, even.

Think for a minute. Have you come across that kind of attitude from another believer? Not just a confidence, but a cockiness? How does that person affect you? Do you admire them? Keep them at a distance? Ignore them most days? Envy them? Why do you think you feel that way? Write down your thoughts and try to be honest.

_____

_____

_____

_____

_____

_____

_____

_____

_____

_____

_____

_____

_____

_____

_____

_____

_____

_____

In this psalm, what at first glance might seem to be swagger is actually a confident assurance that has nothing to do with David (the writer of this psalm) or his talents and abilities, but everything to do with God and his faithfulness.

Pay close attention to verses 5–6. What are the things David is confident God "will do" when days of trouble come around? Because we all know that facing trouble is not a matter of *if*, but *when*.

_____

_____

_____

_____

_____

_____

_____

_____

_____

_____

It Might Interest You to Know

Tradition ascribes Psalm 27
to King David, possibly written
early in his life when there was tension
between himself and King Saul.

GETTING REAL

What's beautiful today?

_____

_____

What's hard right now?

_____

_____

Where do you need God most?

_____

_____

Get real with God by writing or sketching out your thoughts or feelings.

Your Turn

Psalm 27 concludes:

¹³ I remain confident of this:
    I will see the goodness of the LORD
    in the land of the living.
¹⁴ Wait for the LORD;
    be strong and take heart
    and wait for the LORD.

Maybe your parents have forsaken you. Or maybe your friends have. Maybe you're finding life right now to be—in the psalmist's word—"oppressive." Maybe false witnesses have whipped up lies and accusations against you that have no basis in truth. As you wait for the Lord, what statement would you make (even if you're not 100 percent confident)? Write out verses 13–14 in your own words—as verse or prose. What would you hopefully declare, and then confidently proclaim?

A Psalm of _____

_____

_____

_____

_____

_____

_____

_____

_____

_____

Joy explodes throughout the book of Psalms like fireworks, and is the most potent anti-missile defense system there is.

LYNN AUSTIN,

Pilgrimage: My Journey to a Deeper Faith in the Land Where Jesus Walked

COME, AND LISTEN

Psalm 34:11–22 (NLT)

11 Come, my children, and listen to me,
  and I will teach you to fear the LORD.
12 Does anyone want to live a life
  that is long and prosperous?
13 Then keep your tongue from speaking evil
  and your lips from telling lies!
14 Turn away from evil and do good.
  Search for peace, and work to maintain it.
15 The eyes of the LORD watch over those who do right;
  his ears are open to their cries for help.
16 But the LORD turns his face against those who do evil;
  he will erase their memory from the earth.
17 The LORD hears his people when they call to him for help.
  He rescues them from all their troubles.
18 The LORD is close to the brokenhearted;
  he rescues those whose spirits are crushed.
19 The righteous person faces many troubles,
  but the LORD comes to the rescue each time.
20 For the LORD protects the bones of the righteous;
  not one of them is broken!
21 Calamity will surely destroy the wicked,
  and those who hate the righteous will be punished.
22 But the LORD will redeem those who serve him.
  No one who takes refuge in him will be condemned.

Many people go to great effort and even expense to try to completely eliminate trouble from their lives. Yet David confesses "the righteous person faces many troubles."

What troubles are you currently facing?

_____

_____

_____

Recall a time when you were brokenhearted or crushed in spirit. What was going on at the time? Did you feel God was near or far?

_____

_____

_____

_____

_____

_____

It Might Interest You to Know

In Psalm 34, the writer assumes the role of *teacher* (v.11). In the Bible's wisdom literature, "children" is understood to mean "students."

GETTING REAL

What's beautiful today?

_____

_____

What's hard right now?

_____

_____

Where do you need God most?

_____

_____

Get real with God by writing or sketching out your thoughts or feelings.

Your Turn

Imagine you're the teacher, and the lesson you're assigned to teach is "How to Fear the Lord." With a roomful of students equipped with pen and paper at the ready to take notes, what would you say? What would you make certain to communicate as they listened?

A Psalm of _____

Come, my children, and listen to me,
and I will teach you to fear the Lord.

_____

_____

_____

_____

_____

_____

_____

_____

_____

_____

_____

_____

_____

_____

_____

_____

_____

_____

If we are to pray well,
we too must discover the Lord to
whom we speak, and if we use the
Psalms in our prayer, we will stand
a better chance of sharing in the
discovery which lies hidden in their
words for all generations. For God has
willed to make Himself known to us
in the mystery of the Psalms.

THOMAS MERTON,
Praying the Psalms

FULL DISCLOSURE

Psalm 40:1-10 (ESV)

TO THE CHOIRMASTER. A PSALM OF DAVID.

¹ I waited patiently for the LORD;
    he inclined to me and heard my cry.
² He drew me up from the pit of destruction,
    out of the miry bog,
  and set my feet upon a rock,
    making my steps secure.
³ He put a new song in my mouth,
    a song of praise to our God.
  Many will see and fear,
    and put their trust in the LORD.
⁴ Blessed is the man who makes
    the LORD his trust,
  who does not turn to the proud,
    to those who go astray after a lie!
⁵ You have multiplied, O LORD my God,
    your wondrous deeds and your thoughts toward us;
    none can compare with you!
  I will proclaim and tell of them,
    yet they are more than can be told.
⁶ In sacrifice and offering you have not delighted,
    but you have given me an open ear.

CONTINUED ON NEXT PAGE

Burnt offering and sin offering
  you have not required.
7 Then I said, "Behold, I have come;
  in the scroll of the book it is written of me:
8 I delight to do your will, O my God;
  your law is within my heart."
9 I have told the glad news of deliverance
  in the great congregation;
behold, I have not restrained my lips,
  as you know, O LORD.
10 I have not hidden your deliverance within my heart;
  I have spoken of your faithfulness and your
  salvation;
I have not concealed your steadfast love and your
  faithfulness
  from the great congregation.

As a rule, many of us self-edit, even when we're sharing fantastic news. It's possible we don't feel we deserve good things, and so we hold back here and there. Or maybe, due to our upbringing, we try to avoid appearing like we're bragging (some would say seeming prideful), and so we give a condensed version and shy away from telling the whole story. Now maybe you're the exception to that rule, but if not, when's the last time you recall not giving full disclosure to what God has done or is doing? What do you remember about that moment? What were you feeling? Thinking?

_____

_____

_____

_____

_____

_____

_____

_____

It Might Interest You to Know

U2 includes Psalm 40
on the track "40" found on
their 1983 album, *War*.

GETTING REAL

What's beautiful today?

_____

_____

What's hard right now?

_____

_____

Where do you need God most?

_____

_____

Get real with God by writing or sketching out your thoughts or feelings.

Your Turn

Let's redeem that memory of when you last gave a condensed version of a fantastic event. Using the first five verses of Psalm 40 as a guide, craft your own psalm of full disclosure. Don't hold anything back. Tell the whole story. And if by chance you start to feel braggy, remember: the truth is you're bragging about God and God's goodness. So, go for it!

A Psalm of _____

_____

_____

_____

_____

_____

_____

_____

_____

_____

_____

_____

_____

_____

_____

_____

_____

_____

_____

_____

We often imagine, wrongly, that the psalms are private compositions prayed by a shepherd, traveler, or fugitive. Close study shows that all of them are corporate: all were prayed by and in the community.... It goes against the whole spirit of the psalms to take these communal laments, these congregational praises, these corporate intercessions and use them as cozy formulas for private solace.

EUGENE H. PETERSON,
Where Your Treasure Is: Psalms That Summon You from Self to Community

NOW AND FOREVERMORE

Psalm 121 (ESV)

A SONG OF ASCENTS.

[1] I lift up my eyes to the hills.
    From where does my help come?
[2] My help comes from the LORD,
    who made heaven and earth.
[3] He will not let your foot be moved;
    he who keeps you will not slumber.
[4] Behold, he who keeps Israel
    will neither slumber nor sleep.
[5] The LORD is your keeper;
    the LORD is your shade on your right hand.
[6] The sun shall not strike you by day,
    nor the moon by night.
[7] The LORD will keep you from all evil;
    he will keep your life.
[8] The LORD will keep
    your going out and your coming in
    from this time forth and forevermore.

"The Lord is your keeper." What thoughts or feelings does that line stir in you? How do you define "keeper"?

_____

_____

_____

_____

_____

When was a recent time you experienced God as your helper, protector, and keeper?

_____

_____

_____

_____

_____

_____

It Might Interest You to Know

"A Song of Ascents" is a title given to fifteen psalms (120–134) that pilgrims would sing on their way *up* to Jerusalem.

GETTING REAL

What's beautiful today?

_____

_____

What's hard right now?

_____

_____

Where do you need God most?

_____

_____

Get real with God by writing or sketching out your thoughts or feelings.

Your Turn

I lift up my eyes to the hills.
  From where does my help come?

For many, this is a very familiar line from the book of Psalms. Try to write a mirrorlike reflection of this psalm (same themes, even imagery), but for yours choose another word besides "keep" or "keeper." Possible synonyms include the following: *retain, save, store, conserve, put aside, honor, stand by, preserve, sustain, watch over, defend, guard.*

A Psalm of _____

_____

_____

_____

_____

_____

_____

_____

_____

_____

_____

_____

_____

_____

_____

THE BOOK
OF PSALMS
INSTRUCTS US
IN THE USE OF
WINGS AS WELL
AS WORDS. IT
SETS US BOTH
MOUNTING AND
SINGING.

CHARLES SPURGEON,
The Autobiography of Charles H. Spurgeon

I'M GOOD

Psalm 23 (NLT)

A PSALM OF DAVID.

¹ The LORD is my shepherd;
　　I have all that I need.
² He lets me rest in green meadows;
　　he leads me beside peaceful streams.
³ He renews my strength.
　He guides me along right paths,
　　bringing honor to his name.
⁴ Even when I walk
　　through the darkest valley,
　I will not be afraid,
　　for you are close beside me.
　Your rod and your staff
　　protect and comfort me.
⁵ You prepare a feast for me
　　in the presence of my enemies.
　You honor me by anointing my head with oil.
　　My cup overflows with blessings.
⁶ Surely your goodness and unfailing love will pursue me
　　all the days of my life,
　and I will live in the house of the LORD
　　forever.

Chances are good you've heard the twenty-third Psalm, either in part or in whole. You've no doubt heard it if you had any religious training as a child. In fact, you may have even memorized it. At the very least, you've heard it at a funeral, whether in real life or as portrayed in movies and on television. David is the psalm's author, and the framing of his relation to God as that of sheep to Shepherd is timeless.

Where do you recall first hearing or noticing this enduring psalm?

_____

_____

_____

Why do you think it has resonated with so many people over such a long time?

_____

_____

_____

_____

It Might Interest You to Know

Psalm 23 ranks as
the best-known of all
the psalms.

GETTING REAL

What's beautiful today?

_____

_____

What's hard right now?

_____

_____

Where do you need God most?

_____

_____

Get real with God by writing or sketching out your thoughts or feelings.

Your Turn

As a shepherd himself, David was very familiar with the image, role, and actions of one who cares for sheep. But for you, sheep and shepherds may be something you've only read about in books. Try your hand at rewriting Psalm 23 using a different image, one you know quite well. The first step is choosing that image, so here's your prompt:

The Lord is my _____

Now keep going, highlighting similar themes of provision and care and danger and death, simply in a new suit, so to speak.

_____

_____

_____

_____

_____

_____

_____

_____

_____

_____

_____

_____

_____

_____

_____

_____

Of all the beloved psalms,
Psalm 23 brings special
comfort as we journey
through the seasons of
life. . . . The psalmist tells
us that our faithful Lord
who refreshes our souls is the
same One who walks with
us through dark times—times
we're tempted to fear.

RUTH CHOU SIMONS,
GraceLaced

GOD KNOWS

Psalm 139:1–14 (ESV)

TO THE CHOIRMASTER. A PSALM OF DAVID.

¹ O LORD, you have searched me and known me!
² You know when I sit down and when I rise up;
   you discern my thoughts from afar.
³ You search out my path and my lying down
   and are acquainted with all my ways.
⁴ Even before a word is on my tongue,
   behold, O LORD, you know it altogether.
⁵ You hem me in, behind and before,
   and lay your hand upon me.
⁶ Such knowledge is too wonderful for me;
   it is high; I cannot attain it.

⁷ Where shall I go from your Spirit?
   Or where shall I flee from your presence?
⁸ If I ascend to heaven, you are there!
   If I make my bed in Sheol, you are there!
⁹ If I take the wings of the morning
   and dwell in the uttermost parts of the sea,
¹⁰ even there your hand shall lead me,
   and your right hand shall hold me.

CONTINUED ON NEXT PAGE

¹¹ If I say, "Surely the darkness shall cover me,
   and the light about me be night,"
¹² even the darkness is not dark to you;
   the night is bright as the day,
   for darkness is as light with you.

¹³ For you formed my inward parts;
   you knitted me together in my mother's womb.
¹⁴ I praise you, for I am fearfully and wonderfully made.

Who is that person you feel knows you—like really knows the real you? How long have you known each other?

_____

_____

_____

_____

_____

_____

_____

The psalmist (David, in this case) asserts that when it comes to knowing you—like really knowing the real you—God wins the contest, hands down. God knows our thoughts, feelings, whereabouts, and even the words we'll speak before we speak them. Knowing someone else has such knowledge can be quite comforting, and at the same time a little unsettling.

It Might Interest You to Know

Hans Christian Andersen,
the author of popular fairy tales,
including *The Little Mermaid* and
Thumbelina, also wrote a short story
titled "*Ved det yderste Hav*"
("The Uttermost Parts of the Sea"), which
features verses 9–10 of Psalm 139.

GETTING REAL

What's beautiful today?

_____

_____

What's hard right now?

_____

_____

Where do you need God most?

_____

_____

Get real with God by writing or sketching out your thoughts or feelings.

Your Turn

The excerpt presented on pages 165-166 ends on this declarative statement: "I praise you, for I am fearfully and wonderfully made." As you practice writing your own psalm, start with that statement and work from there. Let that declaration be your first step, and then see how things unfold. It's not so much a catalog of how wonderful you are, but rather lines of praise for how wonderful God is—his vast knowledge and authority and power and, above all else, love.

A Psalm of _____

I praise you, for I am fearfully and wonderfully made . . .

_____

_____

_____

_____

_____

_____

_____

_____

_____

_____

_____

_____

_____

_____

_____

IN PSALM 139, WE READ THAT
GOD KNOWS US AND STILL
CALLS US BELOVED. GOD
KNOWS OUR THOUGHTS
AND STILL HOLDS ON TO THE
SAME DIVINE DREAM FOR OUR
LIVES, UNCHANGED SINCE WE
WERE CREATED. EVEN WITH
ALL OF OUR WEAKNESSES,
GOD DOESN'T RUN FROM US.
BECAUSE OF GOD'S NEARNESS,
WE ARE NEVER ALONE.

LISA SHARON HARPER,
The Very Good Gospel

GETTING REAL

Get real with God by writing or sketching out your thoughts or feelings.

Primary Sources

Brueggemann, Walter. *Praying the Psalms.*
    Eugene, OR: Cascade Books, 2007.
Buechner, Frederick. *Wishful Thinking.* San
    Francisco, CA: HarperOne, 1993.
Lamott, Anne. *Help, Thanks, Wow.* New York,
    NY: Riverhead Books, 2012.
Merton, Thomas. *Praying the Psalms.*
    Collegeville, MN: The Liturgical Press, 2014.
Peterson, Eugene H. *Answering God.* San
    Francisco, CA: HarperOne, 1991.

Credits

Text by John Blase